Its Promising Branches

Vivian Kearney

Its Promising Branches
©2017, Vivian Kearney, Benjamin Anzak,
Ian Kearney
Cover illustration © 2017, Vivian Kearney
Illustrations © 2017, Vivian Kearney
Pukiyari Publishers

ISBN-10: 1-63065-072-2
ISBN-13: 978-1-63065-072-8

PUKIYARI PUBLISHERS
www.pukiyari.com

Dedicated to my dear soul mate, Milo, our families, children, grandchildren, friends and our inspiring teachers and mentors and our very helpful editor, Ani Palacios.

With many thanks to two of our five awesome grandsons - Benjamin Anzak and Ian Kearney for their poems included in this collection.

With gratefulness to the teachers, administrators, coaches, assistants, counselors, secretaries, nurses, librarians, workers and staff who work so hard to prepare a good future for all students.

Table of Contents

CONCERNS

Concerned

Let us now be concerned about learning
In these days when memory is an app

When false facts float around
Waiting to be corralled
And shaped into marching songs for armies

Against
Equalizing, liberating,
Public school
Education

Go Public Schools

Public school
The brave, the noble, the benevolent
Ideal of giving everyone a ladder

So we can all meet together
In lands of necessary knowledge

Climbing up from our
Sometimes unfairly
Weathered histories

Is being questioned, disparaged, diminished
By some lords of the game

Calling: Take those private vouchers
Leave those populist ideals
Go for individual dreams
Of Wall Street and beyond
Win much treasure for yourself
Your bootstraps will take you there

Instead of identifying
With public classes
Or Main Street
Academe

The Big Picture

However
In fact there are
How many more programs
Subjects, activities
Accommodations, opportunities
Equipment, materials, facilities
Curricula in place
Tested and improved
For how many decades

Why
Should we
Give up such
A good public deal
And re-invent for private use
A not-so-squeaky wheel

FACILITY

Building Towards Futures

Dancing, scurrying in the patio breeze
Brown and yellow leaves, vari-patterned
Now they skip, twirl and chase each other
Now they rest from all that windy bother

While purple flowers stately watch
Coral companions bloom in the cool sun
In rectangular beige planters contained
Gladly glowing after welcomed rains

Red and white brick walls keep order
Creating meditating spaces outside
Education ruling in the humming school building
May all its denizens be blessed with wise learning

Let's Gather in the Courtyard

The birds in the courtyard trees
Confer and twitter
Whistle and call
In the bright warm
Winter air

Competing with
Louder than
The lunchtime
Chattering students below

Vivian Kearney

School Lyric

The classes – the words
The chairs, desks – the letters
The halls and stairs – the grammar
The cafeteria – the tune-ups
The teachers – the conductors
And the music, the songs
Go on

Empty Classroom

Neon lights hum peaceably
Computers stare silently
Soon to be overtaken by
Students chatting knowingly

Vivian Kearney

Second Language Learners

Those who left
The sandy, sunny
Or rain soaked, windy
Makeshift school spaces

Without any walls, boards
Amenities, facilities

Where they once tried
To learn
In a circle
Rote repeating
So earnestly
Their supplies mostly
Good memories

Now acquiring
Our language
Our culture
So quickly

How did they feel
At first
About those strange halls
Rooms, windows, computers, desks,
Boards, books, materials, doors
Papers galore

TEACHING, LEARNING

Once, Unexpectedly

Once, unexpectedly
Gifted with
Its maroon and gold tomes
The Book of Knowledge encyclopedia
Took me down
So many interesting paths
Of topics to be toured
Eclectically

Now that printed project
Is brought to life
When I visit
Classroom compartments
Of subjects to be heard, learned, tested
Systematically

School can really be
A gift that keeps on giving
A studies paradise
A garden to explore

With our left
And right brains
Evermore

Learning Tree

The learning
Spreads out
In all directions
Dear students,
I just try
To show you how
To hop along
Its promising branches

How, When, Where, What, Why

Discernment, what do you discern?
Sight, what do you see?
Hearing, what do you hear?
Walking, where do you walk?
Learning, what do you learn?

That so much is interesting
That one lifetime cannot suffice
To understand our planet and universe
Or even completely know
One corner of one house

Evolution by Education

Atoms rearrange, why can't souls
Thought evolution matters for each role
Learning, let me use new neural pathways
Let impulse be guided, edified, come what may

Do You Care

Teaching is a highwire act
All eyes shouldn't be but are
Focused on you
Do you know
Do you care
Do you dare
Minds to learn
And keep the pace
And peace besides

Mentors and Teachers

What happened
To that dear old school building
Reigning way up
On yonder hill
In my nostalgic dreams

It was replaced
By other landmarks
Trees and stores
Streets and developments
Parking lots
And further sky

What happened to
Our mentors, teachers
Beacons beckoning,
Encouraging us
To brave journeys
Placing treasured books
In our backpacks
In passing
Not even asking
For later updates

Off they went
Into the unknown blue
While we pondered
Our next paths and stages

Vivian Kearney

Teachers Ubiquitous

Has anyone
Prayed for you
Hoped for
Your continued progress
In sympathy

Many
Of your teachers have
Most probably

Their sayings, advice
Maybe forgotten
Still guide your way
Liberally

Benevolent Encouragement

Go ahead
Let's move
Outside the box
Of self containment
Above the screen
Of I-entertainment
Open the doors
Of development

And get prepared
To make good use
Of capabilities
To learn myriad subjects
In a place of
Multiple diversity

Twelve Year Start

I know, I realize
Right now
You may be asking
Why am I still here
In these boxy classrooms
For so long

But soon, soon
Maybe now
You'll realize
What this present contains
And what its use
Gifts and blessings
Lifelong

SOME SUBJECTS – LITERATURE

Literature

Literature
For sure
Widens your world
Forever

For never
Are you the same
After the rhythm and rhyme
Discussions and stories
Themes, verses and lines
Ideas, observations, comparisons

All made with moving
Picturing words

A true
Jacob's ladder
To the singing stars

Novel Physics

Now we find out
That maybe
Parallel universes
Do exist

And we'll be able to visit
Our other possible stories
Practice for our real lives
After school

Surprise!
It's here already
Virtual reality...

Novels

Vivian Kearney

Reciting Revival

Hamlet came back
His speech practiced
Recited for an English class

And there was that angst again
And convoluted wondering about
A land

From whose bourne
No traveler
Ever returns

Space Travel

A book is a rocket
Sent into orbit
When read
Bringing clothes,
Food for thought,
Blankets for warmth,
Shoes for unknown terrains
From one planet
To another

Word Search

You can play hide and seek
And paint tag
With words

In forests of
Dictionaries, thesauri
Rhyming lists

When one finally
Lets itself be caught

How it shines
In fields of sentences
Let out
From caves of thought

Relating to Poems

The line breaks
Where the heart aches
Where the soul pauses
Where the mind waits

The poetry weaves
Strands of tears
Sparkles of stars
Storms of fears

And peace descends
Hope sings again
And the air vibrates
With echoing amens

Nectar Wise

Dear Emily Dickinson
Were you ever a sufferer
Of insomnia, is that
How you wrote your poems
Into the night

Into the day
Light abuzz with bees
Flowers and butterflies

With your drive
To philosophize, nectar wise
And be understood, cherished
Forever

Teaching Sonnets

While hearing a line in your head, write it down
If you think of a rhyme, note it to the side
A missing word in a thesaurus can be found
If you start an image, with it abide

Use parallelism, metaphor, simile
Without a doubt your poem will be fine
Personification, rhyme, rhythm, hyperbole
Be careful writing each word, every line

Friendship and rivers, music, rain and love
Sweet pets, good food that brings forgotten thoughts
Your family, feelings, guidance from above
Great dances, places, more description than plot

In sonnet form show that for this subject you care
In Shakespeare's manner, memories you'll share

Vivian Kearney

Hand to Heart to Hand

The wonders of writing with your whole hand
A soul, heart and mind connection

With fireflies of letters grouping together
To form flashlights of words, lamps of sentences

So you can build a spirit cabin
Where your mind can find relaxation

Whence your heart can greet each day's
Work, preparations, goals and missions

Blessed Cursive

Pen or pencil lines
Let's not get away from
Your linear transportation

Or lose your paths of discoveries
Ultimately mirroring
God's string composition

School Story

Pinocchio is really
All about school
As well as life lessons

About finally escaping
Distraction's pull
Pleasure islands' traps
Dictator's lies

About receiving
The joys of becoming
A real rescuing *mentsch*

Able to use apt tactics
With caring ingenuity

11 Cinderella Stories from Around the World

Cinderella, the kind, the lovely, the fair
No matter what color her eyes, skin or hair
Suffered, then received reprieves and graces
From many archetypes of people and places

Then what about the historical Louise de Lorraine
Was her story a true model or a mythical salvation
With an improbable prince who did ask for her hand
(And in real life left it again and again)

So, even if at first unfairly hassled
Will we search until we find God's castle?
Isn't it the greatest redeeming romance
When God Himself asks us to an eternal dance?

LEARNING FROM HISTORY

Relational Atoms

The past
If pained
Let it be
As yesterday's rains

The present
Lent for
The moment
Yet all stays

The waves
Of communications
Though abate
Still vibrate

The archetypes
Become teachers
Lights erudite
Mentors forever

Prehistoric

Hands paint-slapped
Onto cave walls

Would you still want to greet us
Reach trustingly across the ages

If you knew the destruction
Our hands were to wield
Eras later

Against your
Ancestral nature

Vivian Kearney

Turning Point

Forgive them all
Said the reviled rabbi
And the train of history
Took another turn

Discovery- Wadi Qumran Scrolls

The sound of breaking pots
By a stone thrown
By a shepherd
Into a Dead Sea cave

Its yawning mouth
Looking like a fanged viper

And the rocks themselves
Moonscape barren

Pitiful the ancient leather
Shredded bindings
Lately discovered
Once trying to protect
Words of scripture

Heartening the smooth
Kindly museum-modern
Displaying cloth

Vivian Kearney

After Movie About Pompei

Why are many historical movies not historical
Evoking away from facts dramatic enough
Not only a business calculation, almost palpable
Aversion to true renditions of times past

Freezing forms artistically
Into statues enveloping humans
Not with marble but in lava and ash
Isn't that a picture of immortality asked

But Vesuvius did happen
And global warming is upon us
Those and coming events are not special effects
But cruel reminders of history's tragedies

Flagships

Nobly adventuring
With their ships
What must
It have been like
For Europeans

To have discovered
For themselves
A whole new world
Of possibilities,
Riches

And what
Did they do with it?

Under their national
And church flags

And where were
The flagless
First inhabitants
Able to keep
Cooperating with nature?

Salons to Revolutions

Mme de Pompadour
So deceptively, demurely
Not ruled but ruling
Organizing salon discussions
Suggesting the right people
For influential places
Tearing at
The fabric of the royal establishment
One of the best
Fifth columns ever sent

When did the aristocracy
Wake up to the fact
That they were being murdered
By someone they had ravished
And the sea, the furious sea
Of anger was out, was out
To displace them
To discredit them
Once those enlightenment
Philosophies were stirred

Alamo

They waited
For Goliad's
Balm of Gilead
Allied aid

They beat their drums
Blew their trumpets
Played their fiddles
Told stories
About getting there

But most were killed
Shouting bravely

Remember!

Vivian Kearney

Truth Frowning

A night cloud of forgetting
Hiding the moonlight of remembering

Every now and then
You do glimpse
The white ravaged orb

Of truth, frowning
At earth events
Under the stars

Ladder

Slowly
The puzzle pieces of human society
Together with all creation
Throughout history
May be fitting together

Hopefully
To form a ziggurat of community
A ladder of consideration
Towards each other

O may it be

WINDOWS OF SCIENCE

Poster to Contemplate

Solar system poster
On a science class wall

Oh, no
It can't be!
That tiny speck

O, yes
Recognize it, retain it
Cope with it

Our planet,
Our world
Is that small

Allow Us

Please, o please
Let us take our turtle
For a walk
Down the hall
We do this all the time
Our teacher lets us

I said, no way
I'm not your teacher
I can't be responsible

And the poor listening turtle
Swam eagerly
Flapped its flippers wavingly
Desperate to get out of its tank
For a while

Class Pet

Little caged guinea pig
With its fluffy fur
Its pleading brown eyes
Whistles its sorrow
Through its buckteeth
Trying to learn the whys
Of its captivity
For the sake of
Human knowledge

You Don't Know

Look at me
Said the tree
Right outside

Branches touching, scratching
The science class window

I bet
You can't tell
Exactly how
I take the sunlight
And photosynthesize

Be ye ever
So wise

PATTERNS AND CHARTS - MATH, LANGUAGES

1 2 3

subject pronouns	
singular	plural
1	
2	
3	

I   un, deux, trois

ℸ, ⅃⅃3, oℷ"ℸc

II   unus, duo, tres

1

2

3

eins, zwei, drei

III   ἑνας, δυο, τρία

∇ uno, dos, tres

O

△

O   uno, due, tre

▽

O

▲

●

▼

●

▲

●

ᴐᵐᵉᵗ, ᴄᴠᴠ, ᴛᴛ

one, two, three

object pronouns	
singular	plural
1	
2	
3	

1 2 3

Keep Those Numbers

Structural
My discipline

A cumulative
Skill like languages
Like music

Kaleidoscopic
The multitude of formulae
Like science

Keep working
On those numbers, algorithms

From first grade
And beyond

And you'll be able
To plan
Rockets to the planets

Houses, bridges, robots,
Cars, I-pads and games
Here on earth

Why Learn a Dead Language

Latin of the clear inflections
The super-influential
In fields of science, law, logic,
Theology, medicine, et cetera
A still living lender

Contrary to the saying
That language didn't kill the Romans
And it won't hurt you

In fact, it will also help
With the real difficulties
Of English phonics, vocabulary
Even English grammar
And its mysterious, confusing
Sparse inflections
Where you can find them

Why a Foreign Language

Why not?
Latin, Spanish, French, German
Most offered in public schools
They're everywhere
In our English words

Be eclectic
And elect all
Then explore even more
So you'll be able
To say why
Multilingually

You'll be a polyglot
By self, immersion, program
Or school taught

You'll be able to travel
Even without transportation
In your mind
And develop other mindsets
In your heart

You can start
Whenever

Though better sooner
Rather than later

ACTIVITIES, AMENITIES

Library

Happy pattering chatter
In the school library
Like bright
Refreshing rain

Thank God for Libraries

Libraries so wise
Comforting throughout my life

First a child minder, story teller
Then a garden of knowledge
Treasure island, horizon expander

A good place to share, to ruminate
To discover true facts
To remember, to reconstitute
So many other geographies, societies
Cultures and lives,
Times historic
Planets and galaxies

Strange Yet Wonderful

Computer system at school
Crashed for a day
Strange the temporary world
Left without electronic organizers
Searchers, page turners,
No web sites, scrolling or googling

Welcome to the library
And the loyal paper media
Of the book world

The Pawn

The pawn
A lowly piece
Some people think
But I say
Why did Fischer win?
Maybe, because of a pawn
Others, they say
That they are pawns themselves
Lowly,
Ignored,
Useless
But I say to those hallowed few
In chess, only a fool
Would give away his pawn
Would lose the match
In the right hands,
Guided by a master
The pawn can be vital
The pawn can be successful
The pawn can be the finisher
The pawn <u>will</u> end the match
In a game of Chess
Should not be ignored
So when you are low
Or feeling like a fool
Just remember the words:
The pawn can turn into a queen, a righteous piece
The pawn, if guided well, will always win the match
Don't despair, you'll make it through, and be the hero, too
--Ian Kearney

Diving Contest

So hello, air,
   And goodbye, fear
I start my graceful falling here.
I swim, I tease,
   I dive with ease
Who cares about the judges' score?
Now I'm a swan
   And swans can soar.

-- Benjamin Anzak

Robotics

Maybe your robot
With good guidance
And modern electronics
Like Doctor Who or Superman
Can help many
Will be used
To show the world
The way to peace

Notes

The droplets of marimba notes
From the music room
Drip down the white wintry halls
Giving a haunting tuneful structure
To the corridors of learning
And to the floating, fleeting
Clouds outside

Music

I listen to music every day
Music is powerful
It can make mighty stubborn kingdoms sway
It can make a mean old king
   let its people free

It can make the everyday drone lighten up
   as a man breathes into his saxophone
It can turn your day from sad to happy
   with just one bar from the neighbor's guitar
It can turn a man like a thorn into a nice one
   with the sweet sound of a horn
It can turn a life as dry as a bone into a slip-and-slide
   with the rolling slurs of a trombone

But don't forget the baritone whose dark and powerful
tone
   is enough to boost any morale
or the collective sounds as you pass the school's
chorale
and the drums with their heartbeat to life
   keeping away all conflicts and strife

Music can help you if you feel down
Music can make friends and family all gather around
Music can turn your dull, mundane world
   into something upside down

-- Benjamin Anzak

Doesn't Make Sense

There are some things that just don't make sense
  like how a turtle can climb a fence
Or like all the math problems on the paper that make
me
  want to yield
Or why the football team is on the marching band
field

-- Benjamin Anzak

Choir

Transported
With you
Moved,
We hear you

Mixing those voices
Blending with those instruments
Powerfully together

Presenting what heartfelt beauty
And musical wisdom

Realistic

I'd like to
Paint
And capture
Last evening's
Backlit
Watercolor
Pink and grey
Sunset clouds

But it wouldn't seem
Believably
Realistic

How do I do this
Dear art teacher

Art Projects in The School Patio

Gigantic metal grasshopper
And other bugs
Wink at students
Through the glass windows
Of the passing halls
Their delicate frames spelled out,
Delineated
Fantastically

Vivian Kearney

It Will Be Fine

It will be fine
It will be okay

You have understanding
Trained nurses and counselors
Principals and secretaries
Many supporters

To help you, advise you
On your way
To a healthy future

TEENAGE LIFE

Scoot

Balancing, scooting, balancing
On the skateboard of teenage life
On the cusp of choices looming
On the sidewalks, goads, roads
Towards adult horizons

Wouldn't You Like

Wouldn't you like
For everybody
To keep everybody
In mind
To talk, act, work, react
Pleasantly
To plan, decide
Wisely, fairly

Nu... (so – well, then)…

Vivian Kearney

Forever Instant

A high school picture
Snapped in the halls of youth
Will the moment be remembered
By two teens
Or their camera

How Modern Your Interests

Gadgeting our ways around the days
Of classes and halls, teachers and pals
Demonstrating how tech-savvy we are
Breathless to drive our very own cars

History, geometry, P.E., algebra, math
Languages, sciences, arts, literature
Even computer courses can't compete
With texted messages and wireless culture

How green, marvelous and modern are your interests
May you use them for opportunities sent
In between the I-phone and information overload
Please heed our lessons and blessings well meant

Vivian Kearney

Down the Halls

Kicking yellow and blue balloons
Down the school's serious halls
Two boys looking for their permanent personae
That will catch up to them
Later or soon

Wasting His Own Time

So sad the wastrel
Drug enhanced or whatever
Noble unto himself
Wasting his own time
Circumventing much concerned counselling
Rejecting all learning paths offered
With none of his own
For his tired, running soul

Special Ed

Let me show you
Blue
O look
How wonderful the sky
Or…yes, you can color it
Red
O see
How fiery, how warm
The orange and yellow sun
Green
Let's paint
The leaves of trees
Let's give your surroundings
School papers
Colors and lines
Profoundly sweet child
By special infancy
Bound

Taking Care of Differences

Kid lies on the floor
Of the school's reception area
Altogether too small
For his gangly feet
Blood on his cheek
Counts and recounts
Baseball cards
Desperately

Some looked at him
No one spoke to him
No one touched him
Until his counselor came
And said, professionally,
Let's go this way

Clearing the place
Which resumed
Normalcy

I Can Also

I am ADD
I branch out
Like a San Antonio oak tree

Not like
An Italian cypress
Or a meditative pine

My leaves can also
Photosynthesize
God's wondrous sun

Multiform Magnets

Wonderful magnet schools
In the ISD systems
Teens responsible already
Know what they will want to do

Even if pulled a little to distractions
Giving youthfulness its due

Starting to walk admirably
In their adult shoes

And

And if not there
There's dual credit
Advanced placement
Offerings

Look at all the efficient ways
You can move
Into your best groove
Faster

SUBSTITUTE

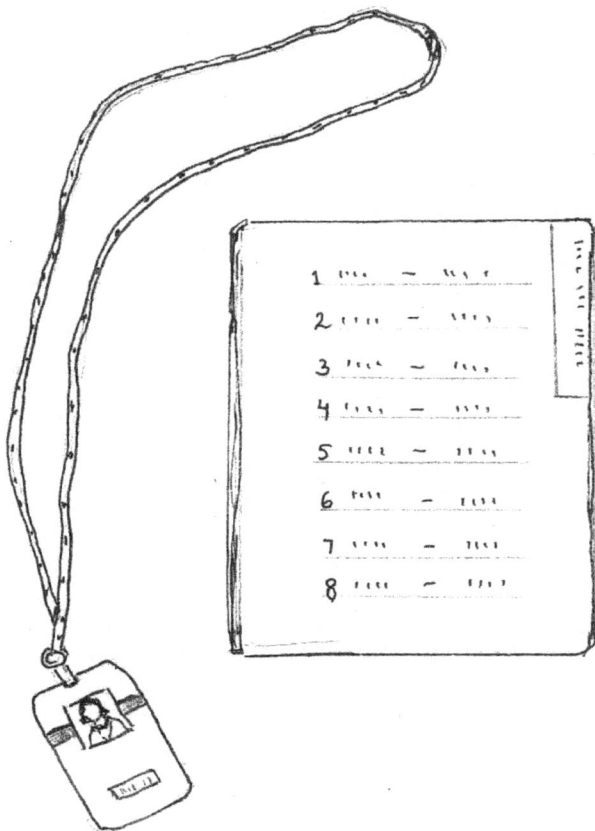

Substituting Is Like Travelling

Given
Your ticket / folder for
The day's travel / job
You run / fly/ walk
With your carry-on
Bag and / or purse

To a needing / needed
City / class
Of math/ science /science /literature / cooking
Computers or other abodes of education

Encountering
Reunions / sympathies / edification
Through corridors
Of nostalgia
Or memory-making moments
In halls / runways revving

To a bright blue unknown
Towards a new stage
Of a young / older age

Call

Eight o'clock and I was going
To the gym, to the cleaners, to stores,
 To do some chores

Eight ten and we rushed out
To get me to a last minute
 Subbing job

Eleven twenty-five
And I'm ensconced now
 In a class interesting and fun

In two time zones at once
 In both universes somehow

Who Are You Today?

Once I was a teacher too
With a complex load of responsibilities
Trundling reams of required language skills
To impart and to grade

Today I'm working out of my box
As I try to decipher
What to do with math papers

Discovering lessons plans
I can tell pupils
To help each other with worksheets
Or take individual tests

While informing the wondering class
About this substitute's protocol

I make myself at home
In your classroom, at your desk
Dear teacher of record

Its Promising Branches

I ask students' names nicely
Then inform them (gently) they will
Be noted with T's for talking
Or NW's for not working
In my own seating chart notebook

But I also record good behavior
Maybe according my signature
On their well-worked papers

I enjoy your decorations, organization
Endeavoring to leave all as found
When I first assumed for an hour, for a day
That I could sit at your desk
Though probably not having
One thousandth of a fraction
Of your numbers knowledge

School Scenes

Leaving the car, marching over the curb
To today's assignment, stepping on
Royalty-hued carpets of leaves, red and gold
Breathtaking when you think this isn't
A seasonal part of the country

Outside the quiet, large windows
Of a waiting empty classroom
White asphalt looks like a whimsical river
Mirroring the white sky
Closer it's a football field
Mathematically lined and numbered

Resting on one prudent leg
The baby turtle in a calculating math class
Is not too sure if it should move
One step forward
Onto the camouflaging rock
Or two steps backwards
Into the gurgling waters
Of the rectangular tank

Conversations

- Why don't you walk with me
And talk with me
Around the gym track
On my road
To graduation

- I perceive
That you must be part of a gang
Said another politely chatting student
Or else why
Would your glasses and purse
Flash with chains?

As I was explaining computer ways
A startling question arose
- Can you be my grandma?
- No, but I can be your substitute,
And nag you into a good class work
And for your happy life silently pray

Another day I was told
- You're a cool substitute
But you lied

You just told my friend
That you speak Spanish
Right after, you said to me
That you speak French

Now, how can that be?

O, the Joys

Guinea pig whistles
With its melancholy eyes pleading
Turtles swim frantically
When they hear students
Asking for permission
To take them for a walk
A tarantula dreams in its jar
That I had thankfully before
Covered with a lid
Shark balloon hovers over my head
Electricity machine gives mild jolts
To warned students and myself

O, the joys
Of science class subbing

Vivian Kearney

Sharp Words, Broken Glasses

I was not kind
Spoke sharply
And later someone tripped
Broke their glasses
And cried

I didn't foresee
Those fragilities
Or consequences

I didn't realize
How much was deposited
In hidden vaults of sadness
On my account

Adding
To another's untold,
Unforgotten failures

Missing
Opportunities for good leading
And learning possibilities

One Encouraging Word

In a
Not quite ready to work
Geography class

One encouraging word
Not costing me much at the time

That made a soul smile
And a sprightly rainbow-colored bird
Of good-will hovered briefly
In the air

Vivian Kearney

A Multiple Subbing Day

Boys leaping, running
With a basketball, symbolizing
What in the world?

A chemical chart on the wall
Students marking paper and skin
With new runes

Learning center's calm
Interwoven with air-conditioning hum
Torn by the bell

Computer games galore
Hieroglyphics sorting, searching,
Internet tests

Happy hosted lunch
With my daughter and other teachers
The day before a springing
Spring break

Mission Accomplished

Write about an act of kindness
Wrote the English teacher in her lesson plan
Done for you, done by you
Who, what, when, where, why and how
Did it your courage renew?

You, restless student, borrowed a pencil, a paper
You threw paper wads disarmingly
You distracted your peers no end
So that they would glow, know gladly
That you are their fun-loving, forever friend

PLAY IT FORWARD

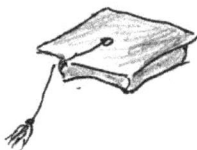

School Year's End

Yellow-brown bonneted sunflowers recede
In the rear-view mirror of my nostalgia
Waving goodbyes, recalling
Sweet-funny-interesting
Learning, teaching,
Substituting times

Play It Forward

Let the good deeds
The surprising care
The shining helpfulness
The continually worked on
Evaluated and checked on
Preparing program
Be passed on
To others

So that
The treasures of
This social ideal
Universal education
Sparkle more and more brightly
Creating cities of joy and beauty
In our land
And other countries

Graduation Exercise

White ribbons of new beginnings
Congratulations hum in the hall
Empty chairs soon to be filled
With students shouting greetings
Their accomplishment
Blazoned on caps
Families yell and whistle in pride

And the instruments tune
And the shuffling prepares
To applaud

OTHER TITLES WITH PUKIYARI PUBLISHERS BY VIVIAN KEARNEY

And yet: A Relationship in Verse (2012 - With Milo Kearney).

Dance with the Red-Gold Sun (2013)

Seeking Signs, Finding Wonders (2014)

The Unfathomable: Holocaust and After (2015)

On God's River of Time (2016)

Bearing Clues - Mysteries of Objects (2017)

Look for them in Amazon.

OTHER TITLES WITH PUKIYARI PUBLISHERS BY MILO KEARNEY

And yet: A Relationship in Verse (2012 - With Vivian Kearney).

Man, God, Satan, Jesus, and Holy Spirit: Poetic Observations (2013)

History's Mysteries in Verse and Sketch (2015)

Don't Read Until 2050: Curiosities from My Memoirs (2015)

Look for them in Amazon.